The Marshall Cavendish

GREEN & PLE

·WALK

CW00369664

The Moorlands of Yorkshire

MARSHALL CAVENDISH

First published in Great Britain in 1997 by
Marshall Cavendish Books, London
(a division of Marshall Cavendish Partworks Ltd).

Copyright © Marshall Cavendish Ltd 1997

ISBN 1-85435-880-4

British Library Cataloguing in Publication Data:
A catalogue record for this book is available from the British Library

Printed and bound in Italy

Some of this material has previously appeared in the
Marshall Cavendish partwork *Out and About*.

While every effort has been made to check the accuracy of these walks, neither Marshall Cavendish
nor Ordnance Survey can be held responsible for any errors or omissions, nor for any consequences
arising from the use of information contained in this book. Marshall Cavendish welcomes readers'
letters pointing out changes that have taken place in land ownership, access, etc,
or inaccuracies in the walks' routes or descriptions.

Picture Credits
Joe Cornish/ National Trust Picture Library page 21. Mary Evans Picture Library page 24. Derek Forss
page 36. Images Colour Library page 25, 41. Milepost 92 1/2 page 28. C. & H.S. Pellant page 17, 20, 32.
Royal Holloway & Bedford New College, Surrey/ The Bridgeman Art Library page 8. Roger Scruton
page 13, 16. Jason Smalley page 9, 12, 29, 37, 40. Simon Warner page 5, 33. All other pictures: Marshall
Cavendish Picture Library

Art Editor: Joyce Mason
Designer: Richard Shiner
Editor: Irena Hoare
Picture Researcher: Vimu Patel
Production: Joanna Wilson

CONTENTS

INTRODUCTION

GREEN & PLEASANT —— WALKS ——

The walks in *GREEN & PLEASANT WALKS* will give you ideas for walks near your own neighbourhood, as well as in other areas of Britain.

All the walks are devised around a theme, and range in length from about 2 to 9 miles (3.25 to 14.5km). They vary in difficulty from very easy to mildly strenuous, and since each walk is circular, you will always end up back at your starting point.

Background information is given for many of the walks, relating legends, pointing out interesting buildings, giving details about famous people who have lived in the area. There are occasional 'Nature Facts' panels, which highlight some of the things you might see in the landscape as you walk.

THE LAW OF TRESPASS

If you find a right of way barred, the law says you may remove the obstruction, or take a short detour.

If the path is blocked by a field of crops, you may walk along the line of the path through the crops in single file. However, in England and Wales, if you stray from the path you are trespassing, and could be sued for damages.

If you do find that your path has been obstructed in some way, report the matter to the local authority, who will take the necessary action to clear the route.

It is illegal for farmers to place a bull on its own in a field crossed by a right of way (unless the bull is not a recognized dairy breed), but if you come across a bull on its own in a field, find another way round – and if you feel sufficiently aggrieved, report the farmer.

USING MAPS

Although this book of *GREEN & PLEASANT WALKS* gives you all the information you need to enjoy your walks, it is useful to have a larger scale map to give you detailed information about

---

THE COUNTRY CODE

- Enjoy the countryside, and respect the life and work of its inhabitants
- Always guard against any risk of fire
- Fasten all gates
- Keep your dogs under close control
- Keep to public footpaths across farmland
- Use gates and stiles to cross fences, hedges etc

- Leave livestock, crops and machinery alone
- Take your litter home with you
- Help to keep all water clean and unpolluted
- Protect wildlife, plants and trees
- Take special care on country roads
- Do not make any unnecessary noise

THE MOORLANDS OF YORKSHIRE

① Marvels of Malham   ⑥ Steam Across the Moors

② Falls and Fells   ⑦ Ancient Lanes

③ View from the Top   ⑧ Ilkley Moor

④ Monks and Methodists   ⑨ Pennine Ways

⑤ Voyage of Discovery   ⑩ Summer Wine Country

All walks featured in this book are plotted and numbered on the regional map below, and listed in the box (left).

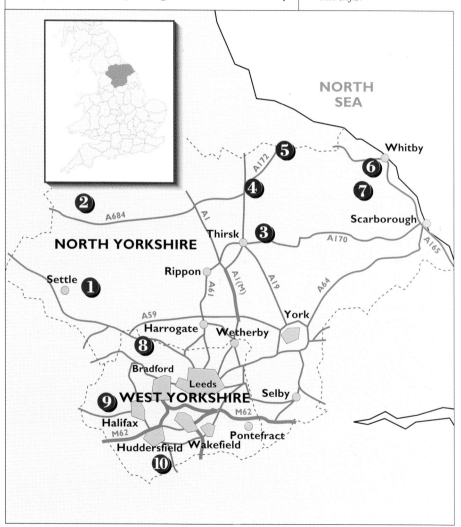

3

The Moorlands of Yorkshire

where you are. Britain is fortunate in having the best mapping agency in the world, the Ordnance Survey, which produces high-quality maps. The most useful of these for walkers are the 1:25,000 Pathfinder, Explorer and Outdoor Leisure maps. Use the grid references given in the fact files to help you find the starting point of each of the walks.

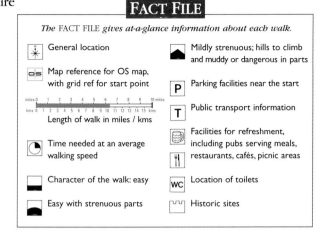

FACT FILE

The FACT FILE gives at-a-glance information about each walk.

	General location		Mildly strenuous; hills to climb and muddy or dangerous in parts
	Map reference for OS map, with grid ref for start point	P	Parking facilities near the start
	Length of walk in miles / kms	T	Public transport information
	Time needed at an average walking speed		Facilities for refreshment, including pubs serving meals, restaurants, cafés, picnic areas
	Character of the walk: easy	WC	Location of toilets
	Easy with strenuous parts		Historic sites

GRID REFERENCES

All Ordnance Survey maps are over-printed with a framework of squares, called the National Grid. This is a reference system which, by breaking the country down into squares, lets you pinpoint an area and give it a unique number.

On OS Landranger, Pathfinder and Outdoor Leisure maps, a reference to an accuracy of 100m is possible. Grid squares on the maps cover an area of 1km x 1km on the ground.

GRID REFERENCES

Blenheim Palace, in Oxfordshire, has a grid reference of **SP 441 161**. This is constructed as follows:

SP: These letters identify the 100km grid square in which Blenheim Palace lies. The squares form the

basis of the National Grid. Information on the 100km square covering any given map is given in the map key.

441 161: This reference locates the position of Blenheim Palace to 100m in the 100km grid square.

44: This part of the reference is the number of the grid line which forms the western (left-hand) boundary of the 1km grid square in which Blenheim Palace appears. It is printed in the top and bottom margins of the relevant map (Pathfinder 1092 here).

16: This part of the reference is the number of the grid line which forms the southern boundary of the 1km grid square in which Blenheim Palace appears. The number is printed in the left and

right-hand margins of the relevant OS map (Pathfinder 1092 here).

Both numbers together (SP 4416) locate the bottom left-hand corner of the 1km grid square in which the Palace appears. The last figures in the reference **441 161** pinpoint the position in the square; dividing its western boundary lines into tenths and estimating on which imaginary tenths line the Palace lies.

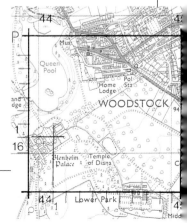

The Marvels of Malham

Through a limestone landscape to a dramatic dry waterfall

This dramatic view shows the imposing cliffs of Gordale Scar.

The village of Malham, in the Yorkshire Dales, is the gateway to an area of great scenic diversity. The geology consists of water-soluble Great Scar limestone, over impermeable Silurian slate. This has created a fine landscape of gorges, crags, lakes and waterfalls.

The circular walk begins in Malham **A** itself. Despite its popularity, the village retains its charm. Behind the Old Smithy, a footbridge leads you out into the open countryside, through a network of small fields, to the waters of Gordale Beck. The path takes you to the dramatic gorge of Gordale Scar **D**, where two waterfalls cascade into a cleft, the shores of the beautiful Malham Tarn **H**, the rock amphitheatre of Malham Cove **L**, and back into town.

THE WALK

MALHAM–GORDALE SCAR–MALHAM COVE

The walk begins from the car park by
the Visitors' Centre in Malham.

1 Leave the car park to find the Old Smithy on your right. Cross Malham Beck on the footbridge behind the smithy and bear right along a well-defined footpath to Gordale Beck. Follow the stream up the same unmistakable path to the woods and waterfall of Janet's Foss **B**, then continue up the path until you come to a road.

2 Turn right along the road, past Gordale Bridge **C**. After 250 yards (225m), just after the road bends to the right, you come to a gate on your left. Go through this and follow the path across a field to enter the rocky ravine of Gordale Scar **D**. Scramble up the tongue of rock in the middle of the lower of the two waterfalls. The hand and footholds are good, but care must be taken, especially if the rocks are wet. Above the lower fall, the path climbs some steps to the top of the gorge.

3 Above Gordale Scar, the path continues to rise gently, before crossing open ground to reach a wooden stile over a stone wall. Seaty Hill **E** is above you to your right. Cross the stile and turn right along a surfaced road. In a short while, Mastiles Lane **F** crosses the route.

4 The road bears left to follow Mastiles Lane, but you go straight ahead along an unsurfaced track, with Great Close **G** ahead and to your right. Follow a path swinging left across the field to follow the edge of a plantation. When you meet a beck issuing from Malham Tarn **H**, continue alongside it to a road.

5 Turn right, go through a gate and over a low bridge. Take the signposted path immediately left to the Water Sinks **J**.

6 Continue alongside a stone wall into a dry, rocky ravine. Leave at the other end by contouring right across an open hillside. Turn left at a signpost towards Malham Cove, crossing a stile over a wall to enter a long, dry valley. At its end, there is another wooden sign.

7 Bear right to cross a limestone pavement **K**. Take care in wet weather, as the clints can be very slippery. After about 150 yards (135m), the pavement ends. Follow a signed path to the bottom of Malham Cove **L**. Continue along the path through the valley bottom, out of the cove onto a surfaced road. Bear left and walk down the road back to Malham village.

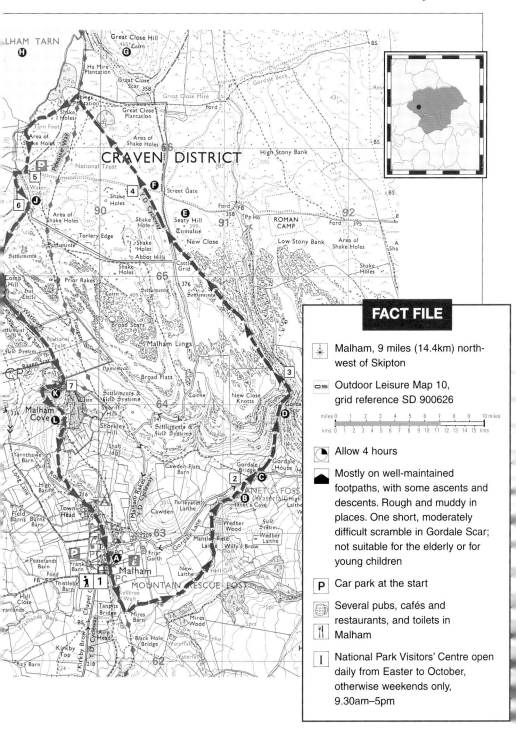

FACT FILE

Malham, 9 miles (14.4km) north-west of Skipton

Outdoor Leisure Map 10, grid reference SD 900626

miles 0 1 2 3 4 5 6 7 8 9 10 miles
kms 0 1 2 3 4 5 6 7 8 9 10 11 12 13 14 15 kms

Allow 4 hours

Mostly on well-maintained footpaths, with some ascents and descents. Rough and muddy in places. One short, moderately difficult scramble in Gordale Scar; not suitable for the elderly or for young children

P Car park at the start

Several pubs, cafés and restaurants, and toilets in Malham

I National Park Visitors' Centre open daily from Easter to October, otherwise weekends only, 9.30am–5pm

Droving Days

Drovers Halt, Island of Mull in the Background
by Richard Ansdell

Before the advent of railways, livestock was moved from place to place 'on the hoof'. Much of this traffic was local, with a few animals being taken to a nearby market, but each year there were longer migrations.

Hardy cattle from Scotland and the North were taken to the pastures of East Anglia for fattening and slaughter, while Welsh animals went to Kent, Essex, and Buckinghamshire. Large herds were built up as animals were traded along the way.

They were taken along time-honoured routes that avoided, as far as possible, roads and towns. They spread out over open country, and met up again at passes or fords.

As they went, the drovers kept up a constant noise — shouting, blowing horns or playing bagpipes. This was partly to keep the cattle moving, and partly to warn farmers of their approach, so they could pen their own beasts before they got caught up in the general movement.

The drovers led nomadic lives. They slept under the stars, only occasionally staying at an inn along the way. As a consequence they often looked quite unkempt, but they were responsible men. Much of the commerce in cattle was done on credit, and farmers relied on drovers to bring back the cash once the beasts were sold.

Drovers had to be licensed, by law. They were entrusted not only with with cattle, but also with letters and financial commissions. Several banks owed their origins to arrangements made for drovers, and in Cromwell's day they were used as tax gatherers.

Falls and Fells

A walk on the moors near a market town in the Dales

The ridge of dramatic North Rakes Hill is highly distinctive.

Wensleydale, which carves a bold path through the heart of the Yorkshire Dales, is characteristically broad and well wooded. During the Middle Ages it was known as Yoredale, after the River Yore, now Ure, which runs through it. The dale's current name comes from the small market town of Wensley at its eastern end.

This walk investigates the area on many levels. It takes in the high tops and limestone scars of North Rakes Hill, complete with sinister swallow holes, going on to wooded dales and field enclosures in the valley bottoms. At the centre of the dale is the small market town of Hawes, which sprang up following the granting of its market charter by William III in 1700.

THE WALK

HAWES–SEDBUSK–HARDRAW
The walk starts from the Upper Dales Folk Museum **Ⓐ**,
just to the east of the town centre in Hawes.

1 Leave car park via access road, turn right, then right again on Brunt Acres Road. About 50 yards (45m) beyond a bridge over old railway line, turn left along farm road, then right on route signed 'Pennine Way'. At end of field path, go through gate; continue on road. Cross river on Haylands Bridge **Ⓑ**. After road bears left, go through stile on right to Sedbusk. Cross bridge and stile to road.

2 Cross, go over stile opposite signposted 'Sedbusk ¼ mile'. Ignore track ahead; instead bear half right towards stile on far wall. Turn left up road to Sedbusk **Ⓒ**. Fork right through village and follow track to 'North Rakes Hill'. Continue up to gate.

3 Climb stile to left just before gate, and head up track. Follow path to right of a small clump of sycamore, then bear left behind them. Continue through gate, then another on right. Follow contours of hill round to waymarker. Bear left along clear track over moor. Beyond next mark, fork left, head over tops.

4 Detour to cairn **Ⓓ** on left for great view. Return to track to continue. Take right fork and head to right of group of cairns in distance. Cross Pike Slack, a small river, and continue; keep close to outcrops on right. Beware of deep swallow holes **Ⓔ**, where becks plunge into underground caves. Go right of five cairns, follow path over moor. Cross Shivery Gill with care. At junction, bear left. Turn left on road. View from Sowry Head **Ⓕ**.

5 After 300 yards (270m), turn right on path to High Shaw. Follow path right of barn, over stile, down hill; keep close to wall, left. At bottom, climb stile, walk along bank; care at point where erosion has narrowed path. Cross next stile, continue 30 yards (27m). Cross stile, left into field. Cross fields to buildings. Take path to right of gate to road. Turn right.

6 After 60 yards (55m), go down steps on left and stay left on path by bank **Ⓖ**. Beyond gate, bear left to minor road. Turn right along main road. After 100 yards (90m) climb stile on right. Walk down farm track. At farm, turn right through stile. Follow path, through stiles and gates, to road. Right to Green Dragon Inn.

7 (To visit Hardraw Force **Ⓗ**, go and return through pub.) Cross road. Follow path right of café, bear left after 50 yards (45m). Path crosses fields and stiles. At road, turn right to Hawes.

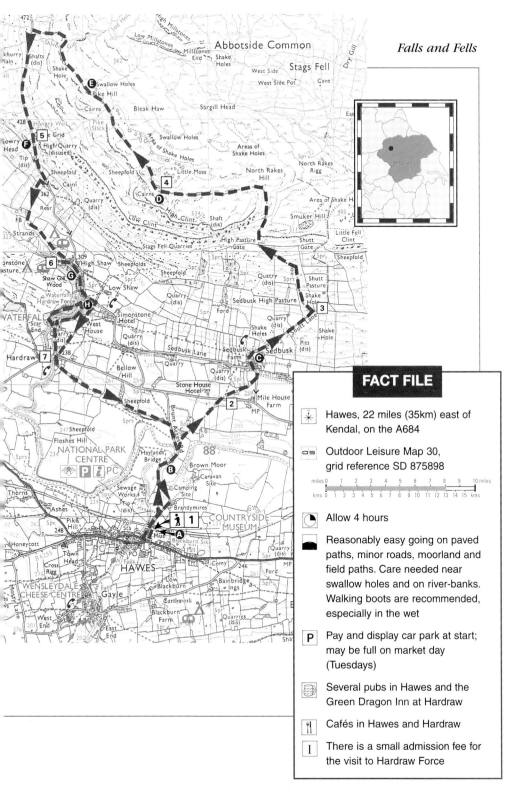

Falls and Fells

FACT FILE

☀ Hawes, 22 miles (35km) east of Kendal, on the A684

⌗ Outdoor Leisure Map 30, grid reference SD 875898

miles 0 1 2 3 4 5 6 7 8 9 10 miles
kms 0 1 2 3 4 5 6 7 8 9 10 11 12 13 14 15 kms

◗ Allow 4 hours

■ Reasonably easy going on paved paths, minor roads, moorland and field paths. Care needed near swallow holes and on river-banks. Walking boots are recommended, especially in the wet

P Pay and display car park at start; may be full on market day (Tuesdays)

🍺 Several pubs in Hawes and the Green Dragon Inn at Hardraw

🍴 Cafés in Hawes and Hardraw

I There is a small admission fee for the visit to Hardraw Force

Hardraw Force

The waters of Hardraw Force spill over a wooded cliff in a solid plume.

After many practice runs over small falls in the woods above, Fossdale Beck plummets 96 feet (29.3m) into the depths of Hardraw Scar, to become England's highest unbroken waterfall above ground. Since Victorian times, the spectacle, which was painted by Turner, has attracted crowds of tourists.

The waters have worn away the soft shale behind the fall, which leaves room for those who dare to walk behind the fall and stare out through the curtain of water.

There is a local tale that tells of a sheepdog that explored a cave behind the fall, and disappeared for a while. The animal then surfaced from the underground system at Cotterdale, totally hairless.

It is entirely due to a previous landowner, Lord Wharncliffe, that we can enjoy the falls today. After a devastating flood washed away bridges and damaged several villages in the area towards the end of the 19th century, the overhanging lip of the Force was totally destroyed, leaving water to spill unceremoniously down the shale cliff of the scar.

Wharncliffe realized what a loss this was and commissioned workers to rebuild the lip, ensuring that Hardraw Force was restored to its former glory.

View from the Top

Walking around the rugged Sutton Bank escarpment

Sutton Bank overlooks Gormire Lake, the Vale of York and the Pennines.

Sutton Bank is undeniably one of the most popular beauty spots of the North Yorkshire Moors. Once they have climbed to the top of the escarpment, walkers can admire Gormire Lake **F**, which glistens like a jewel. Westward, across the vales of York and Mowbray, there is a stunning panoramic view of the rugged Yorkshire Dales.

The circular walk leads through open farmland and around an extensive area of grassland gallops used for training racehorses. The return to Sutton Bank follows part of the Cleveland Way, which is one of the Countryside Commission's designated national walking trails.

The skies above Sutton Bank are often busy with gliders that soar overhead on

Continued on p. 16➡

13

THE WALK

SUTTON BANK
The walk starts from the eastern car park at the top of Sutton Bank.

1 From the rear (eastern) car park, walk to the exit/entrance junction with the main road (A170). Turn left, signposted Scarborough, and walk along the roadside grass verge.

2 Walk along the front edge of the Hambleton Inn **A** car park, which then leads to a narrow lane, signposted Cleveland Way, running parallel with the main road. Follow this lane as it bends left and then enters a woodland area.

3 Continue ahead, past the driveway entrance to Hambleton House **B**. Beyond the driveway, the Cleveland Way turns right, but you should continue ahead. This part of the route follows an ancient highway **C**. Follow the signpost for Dialstone. The route leads through the gap in the white wood fencing and over the bark-laid horse track. Follow the grass track ahead with the old limestone wall on your right. Walk across the driveway entrance to Hambleton High House, and continue ahead walking in the direction of the radio mast.

4 At the road junction, take the road signposted for Boltby and Hawnby. After 50 yards (45m) turn left and walk along the driveway to Dialstone Farm **D**. As you approach the farm entrance, turn left and follow the public bridleway sign, with the fence rail that encloses the horse gallops on your left.

5 Near the disused quarry, the track makes a double bend. Follow the sign for Jennett Well, keeping the stone wall and quarry on your left.

6 Bear right past the group of wind-blown Scots pines, and cross over the stile to turn left along the escarpment edge. As you walk along the escarpment you can enjoy the vista, which includes Gormire Lake **F**.

7 Either return to the car park or make a short detour to cross the busy main road (taking great care). Walk to the escarpment edge to see White Mare Crag **E** and to enjoy the splendid panorama that makes this viewpoint so popular.

Nature Facts

Masham sheep. This breed of sheep is popular in the dales.

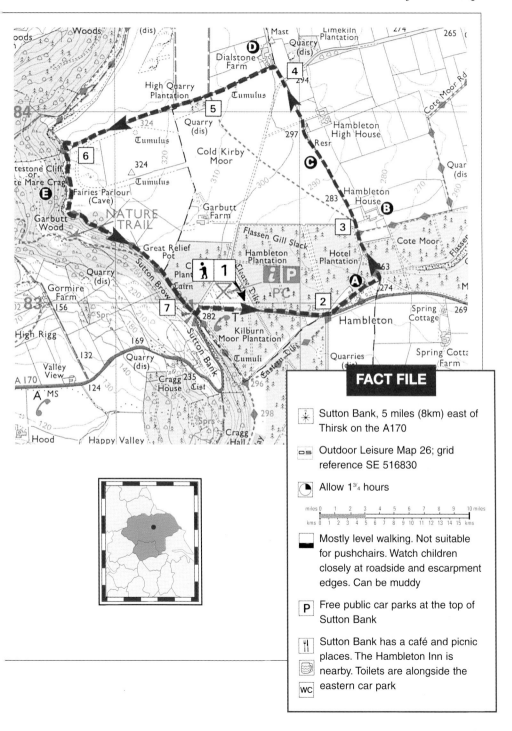

FACT FILE

☀ Sutton Bank, 5 miles (8km) east of Thirsk on the A170

⬛ Outdoor Leisure Map 26; grid reference SE 516830

◔ Allow 1³⁄₄ hours

miles 0 1 2 3 4 5 6 7 8 9 10 miles
kms 0 1 2 3 4 5 6 7 8 9 10 11 12 13 14 15 kms

⬛ Mostly level walking. Not suitable for pushchairs. Watch children closely at roadside and escarpment edges. Can be muddy

P Free public car parks at the top of Sutton Bank

🍴 Sutton Bank has a café and picnic
📖 places. The Hambleton Inn is nearby. Toilets are alongside the
WC eastern car park

strong up-currents and rising pockets of warm air. The Yorkshire Gliding Club, established in 1931, has its station and airfield on the remarkably flat stretch of land above the semi-circle of very steep cliffs. This natural amphitheatre creates thermals, and funnels the prevailing westerly winds into up-currents.

The flat limestone lands of the Hambleton Hills around Sutton Bank provide excellent conditions for horse racing. The sport was well established as long ago as 1612. Racegoers sought refreshment at the Hambleton Inn ❶ and Dialstone Inn (now Dialstone Farm ❶). The name of the farm probably originates from the dial or weighing machine used to weigh in the jockeys. In 1755 the main prize, 'The Hundred Guineas', was transferred to York, and as a result the local races went into decline. However, the tradition continues with the stables at Hambleton House ❸ and the use of the gallops for training.

Hambleton House, with its racing stables, lies at the foot of the Hambleton Hills.

Gormire Lake is the only natural lake of any significant size in the North York Moors. Its formation is thought to date from the end of the Ice Age, when part of a meltwater channel was blocked by a landslide at the edge of the escarpment. Local people tell a tale that suggests that the lake is bottomless, and say that it is haunted by a white mare and its rider, who years ago plunged to their watery grave from the cliffs above.

The 70 feet (21m) of vertical cliff-face that rises above Gormire Lake is referred to as White Mare Cragg ❸, or Whitestone Cliff. After a rockfall in 1755, the freshly revealed limestone face was said to have the appearance, from a distance, of a white horse. A nature trail circles the lake, which is a breeding place for wild duck, coots and the great crested grebe.

The Drove Road

A part of this walk follows an ancient highway ❸ that was once used by Scottish cattlemen (drovers, *see page 8*). In the 18th and 19th centuries they drove their cattle 'on the hoof' into England to sell in the expanding market and industrial towns. The 15 miles (24km) of highway that runs between Sutton Bank and Osmotherley is known as the Hambleton Drove Road, and the weary drovers would have quenched their thirst at the Hambleton or Dialstone Inn.

Monks and Methodists

A country walk round a non-conformist village and a catholic chapel

Cattle graze in the stone-walled fields above Osmotherley.

This walk, at the edge of the North York Moors National Park, gives a flavour of the varied natural habitats of the region: conifer plantations and mixed woodland; fields and open moorland; a reservoir and a clear stream. At its heart is the picturesque village of Osmotherley, and its legacy of religious and secular buildings.

North of the village, where the walk begins, is Cod Beck Reservoir **A**. It was created for the Yorkshire Water Board in 1953. A stone quarry was submerged, as were some cottages at Wild Goose Nest, where there was once an illicit still.

You head across open moor onto an old, straight track through a plantation of conifers. Green Lane, bordered by rowan,

Continued on p. 20➤

17

THE WALK

COD BECK RESERVOIR—OSMOTHERLEY

The walk starts at a small car park at the north end of Cod Beck Reservoir **Ⓐ**, opposite a standing stone marked 'Lyke Wake Walk'.

1 Follow a small path down to the stream and cross the stepping stones (after heavy rain, walk along the road away from the reservoir, cross the footbridge, then return on the other bank of the stream). Continue uphill, with a plantation to your right. Climb a ladder stile into the plantation, and follow the main track ahead between the trees. When the plantation ends, continue ahead on the same track for nearly ¾ mile (1.2km) until you reach a sign for the Cleveland Way.

2 Pass through a squeeze stile to your right, to join the Cleveland Way. Follow this broad track gently downhill, passing to the right of a house and crossing stiles. At the bottom of the hill, cross a footbridge waymarked with an acorn. Continue on the Way, uphill through trees and across fields to a lane. Cross this and pass between two cottages, with a Methodist chapel **Ⓑ** on your right. Go under an archway to the main street. There is an old market cross **Ⓒ** across the road.

3 Turn left along the street, then right along School Lane to the church **Ⓓ**. Return to the main street and turn left. Continue ahead, past the Old Hall **Ⓔ**. At the end of the village, turn left down Ruebury Lane on the Cleveland Way. Shortly after passing the last house on your right, turn right on a path signposted to the Lady's Chapel. Where the track ahead is marked 'Private', go left up some steps to the chapel **Ⓕ**.

4 Go past the chapel and follow a path downhill alongside a wall to your left, until you reach the Cleveland Way. Turn right. Follow the Way ahead into a wood. Bear right at the fork a little way into the trees. Continue ahead past the BT station **Ⓖ**.

5 About 200 yards (180m) beyond a trig point, go through a gate and across a stile. Turn right and follow a peaty path downhill, through the heather and back to the start.

Nature Facts

Mayfly. A creature that starts life in water as a 'dun', pursues a brief life on land, breeds, then dies.

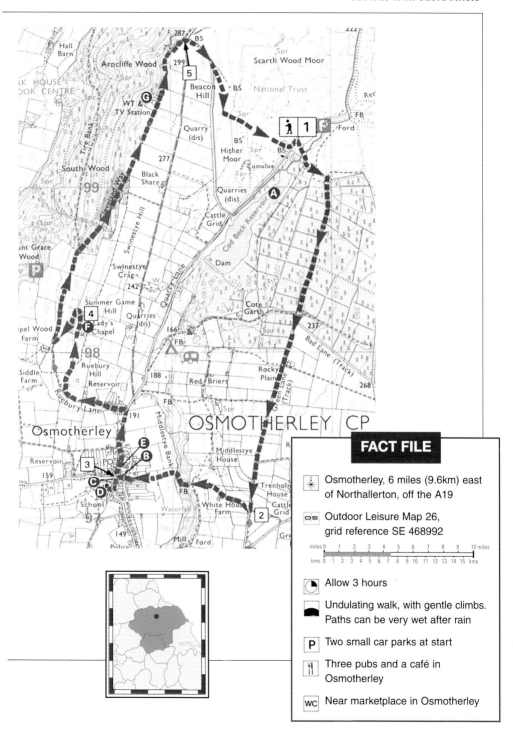

FACT FILE

Osmotherley, 6 miles (9.6km) east of Northallerton, off the A19

Outdoor Leisure Map 26, grid reference SE 468992

Allow 3 hours

Undulating walk, with gentle climbs. Paths can be very wet after rain

P Two small car parks at start

Three pubs and a café in Osmotherley

WC Near marketplace in Osmotherley

honeysuckle, dog roses, hawthorn and gorse, descends gently out of the trees. There are good views of Osmotherley to be seen to your right.

The route turns off to follow the Cleveland Way. This, Britain's second oldest long-distance path, is a well marked route that runs 93 miles (150km) from Helmsley to Filey Brigg.

You cross Cod Beck and pass through woods to Osmotherley. The village has many connections with John Wesley. He was invited here in 1745 by Peter Adams, a former Franciscan friar.

The chapel **B** in Chapel Passage, built in 1754, is one of the earliest non-conformist chapels in England, and is still in use today.

John Wesley often preached here; he used to stand up on a stool because he was short, and it made it easier for the congregation to see him. The stool is still in the chapel.

Wesley preached from the stone market stall by Osmotherley's market cross.

The market cross **C** was erected in 1874 to replace an ancient one, the top of which can be seen outside No. 12 West End. A Saturday market was held here until 1823.

The Church of St Peter **D** stands on the site of a pre-Norman building, stones from which can be seen in the porch. The font and doorway are Norman, and date from around 1190, but much of the church was destroyed by Scottish raiders in 1322 and restored in 1350. An interesting feature is part of an ancient tombstone, its ends supported by a carved bear.

The Old Hall **E** in North End was bought by Lady Juliana Walmsley in 1665, for the Franciscan friars. They had to leave in 1832, but returned in 1969. The top floor is now a Catholic church.

The friars served pilgrims visiting the Chapel of Our Lady of Mount Grace **F**, which stands on a hilltop outside the village. It was built by Carthusian monks from Mount Grace Priory early in the 16th century, on the site of an earlier shrine, and rebuilt in 1960. The large, well-preserved ruins of the priory, which was founded in 1398, stand at the bottom of the hill, west of the route.

As you head north on the Cleveland Way, you pass a BT radio station **G**, 982 feet (299m) above sea level. As you reach the end of the walk you cross moorland. Red grouse and curlews may be seen, while lizards live among the bracken. Hares are common on the hillside that you cross as you return to the start.

Voyage of Discovery

Through the countryside where Captain Cook spent his childhood

Roseberry Topping dominates the flat expanse of Great Ayton Moor.

This walk through the scenic North Yorkshire countryside connects five places associated with the early life of Captain James Cook.

The farm where he lived for eight years still nestles at the foot of the moor; All Saints' churchyard **C** in Great Ayton contains the grave of his brothers and sisters, and the school where he was educated is still standing. It now houses an interesting collection of Cook memorabilia.

The walk also offers spectacular views across the Cleveland Plain to the hills at the edge of the North York Moors. The county of Cleveland is due north.

From viewpoint **B** you can see the village of Marton, where Cook was born. The site of his birthplace is set in a park.

THE WALK

LITTLE AYTON–GREAT AYTON
The walk begins at Gribdale Gate car park.

1 From the grid take Cleveland Way path into forest. Pass through gate, up track between trees. Steps to monument **A** and view **B**.

2 With back to inscription on monument, look right, to gateposts at 100 yards (90m). Pass through, to worn track. Pass small quarry on left. Path goes down, broken wall on left. At end of wall, path splits; take right fork, down through trees to a forest road, turn left. Continue until you round a sharp right bend; proceed 250 yards (225m). Through a gate to a wall corner 50 yards (45m) beyond.

3 From the corner go straight on path; follow top edge of field to gate into lane, wire fence both sides. Lane becomes tarmac road; follow to turn left through gate marked 'Fir-brook'.

4 Lane passes through gates, over railway line, descends to Little Ayton, to right of buildings.

5 At junction, right, away from bridge. At far end of first house on left, turn left along signed path to bridge. Right across the field on faint path; bear right again on path across next field to stile. Continue on clear path across field. Path follows hedge on right past sports field into village.

6 Left on High Street to the road junction beside the bridge.

7 Go down opposite road (Low Green); second road on right to church **C**. Return. Cross bridge, ahead to obelisk in garden, left, site of Cook's father's cottage **D**. Return. Retrace steps. Beyond bridge is museum **E**. Continue on left past

pub, left at junction, soon right through gate in wall.

8 Path leads through gates, through copse, straight to railway line. Cross; continue to junction of tracks. Stile opposite, walk with fence left. Keep fence left; stile to wood.

9 Climb to junction; right, then left and through wood. Cross stile to field; left, with fence on left, to stile. Right, away from stile, along top of field. Cross stile, keep fence on right to next stile.

10 Cross; right to farm **F**. At the junction, straight ahead,

left of farm. Join road
hrough wood.

11 Left at junction.
Do not go left at
'phone box, but ahead,
behind houses. End of
terrace, right to stile; left,
with fence on left, to
stile. Continue ahead to
metal gate on left. Left,
then right along fence
back to car park.

**Woody nightshade, a
scrambling perennial**

FACT FILE

☀ Great Ayton, 5 miles (8km) from
Guisborough

os Pathfinder 601 (NZ 41/51), grid
reference NZ 591110

miles 0 1 2 3 4 5 6 7 8 9 10 miles
kms 0 1 2 3 4 5 6 7 8 9 10 11 12 13 14 15 kms

◑ Allow 4½ hours

◼ Gradual ascent to Easby Moor, but
steep descent through a wood.
There is a steady climb
through a wood towards Airy
Holme Farm

P Gribdale Gate car park, 2 miles
(3.2km) east of Great Ayton

☕ Inns, cafés, shops in Great Ayton

WC By the Captain Cook Schoolroom
Museum

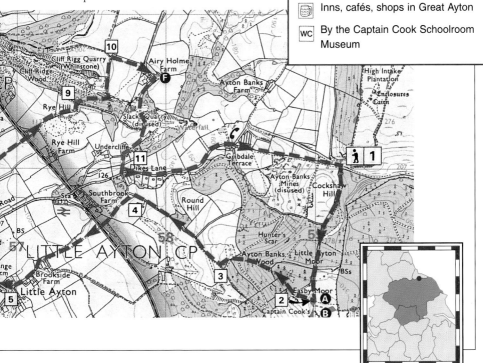

Captain James Cook R.N., F.R.S.

Portrait of Cook by Nathanial Dance (1735-1811). (National Maritime Museum)

James Cook (1728–79) rose from humble beginnings as a farmer's son to become the greatest seaman of his time.

He started as an apprentice on a collier, transporting coal to and from Whitby, and it was a Whitby ship that he chose to take on his three great voyages of exploration. During these voyages he dispelled the myth of the existence of a great southern continent. He accurately charted and explored the whole coastline of New Zealand and the eastern coast of Australia, and was the first navigator to explore the Antarctic region.

On his final voyage he searched for the mythical North West Passage between the Pacific and Atlantic Oceans across northern Canada.

Cook first came to the attention of the Navy when his survey of the St Lawrence river in Canada enabled British forces to capture Louisberg and Quebec from the French. But on his first great voyage of exploration it was as an astronomer that he was sent to Tahiti, to observe the transit of Venus across the sun.

He also experimented successfully with combating scurvy, a disease caused by lack of vitamin C, among his sailors. He did this by giving his men fresh vegetables and fruit to eat on their long sea voyages. His paper on the subject won him the Royal Society Gold Medal.

During most of his time in the Pacific, Cook got on well with the local people, but due to a misunder-standing over a missing boat, he was killed. He was mourned not only by his crew but by the people of Hawaii, who gave him a chief's funeral.

Steaming Across the Moors

Railways and waterfalls in superb moorland countryside

Goathland lies in a beautiful moorland setting, bright with colour in summer.

Goathland, in the North York Moors National Park, is an ancient settlement surrounded by moorland some 500 feet (150m) above sea level. In late summer, the stone buildings bask in a sea of purple heather.

From the time of Henry III to the present day, the common land in and around the village has belonged to the Duchy of Lancaster. Today, many of its visitors come to see the steam trains of the North Yorkshire Moors Railway, which stop at the station here.

The route goes around the village, but it is worth exploring the centre before you start. The houses edge a wide street with grassland on either side, kept neat by black-faced sheep, which wander freely.

THE WALK

GOATHLAND–DARNHOLME
The walk starts at Goathland's church.

1 Cross road and take footpath to right of hotel, signed to Mallyan Spout. Path descends steeply to river. Follow the waymarked footpath left to view waterfall **B**, then retrace your steps and follow the path signposted to Beck Hole. You head uphill, with river below on left, and eventually drop steeply again to Incline Cottage **C**.

2 Bear left and follow the main track. Go through gate on right, then along lane. Pass through gate and turn left along road. Continue through hamlet of Beck Hole **D**. Road curves sharp right, up steep hill. Just beyond the railway line, take the lane right, to Hill Farm.

3 By farm, take main path right (surfaced with chippings). Follow farm track past a cottage to natural amphitheatre in hillside. Keep to path across hillside, with river and Water Ark Foss **E** in trees below on right. Descend to footbridge over river and under the railway. Climb steps opposite and cross stile at top. Turn left along edge of field. Climb stile and follow narrow lane to gate to a road.

4 Left, and continue to the crossroads at Darnholme. Left through village and down across railway. Cross Eller Beck at ford with stepping stones. Take path right, along valley, climbing steeply up steps by the railway line. With wall on right, follow the path to Goathland Station **F**.

5 Go through gate to visit station, then rejoin path, which climbs along valley side and curves left by a group of cottages, to a road. Cross, continue ahead down a tarmac lane almost opposite, until farm is directly on your right.

6 Take the signposted footpath diagonally right, downhill, over a waymarked stile, down a narrow valley. At lower end, cross a footbridge. Go through gate to right of bungalow, and cross another footbridge. Keep right of farm buildings and go through the gate.

7 Pass under railway bridge, continue past Abbot's House up lane. At junction with the disused railway, continue ahead into camping field. With hedge on left, continue to end of the field. Climb stile and turn right, then climb another stile. Follow the obvious path across fields to emerge on green by church, where the walk began.

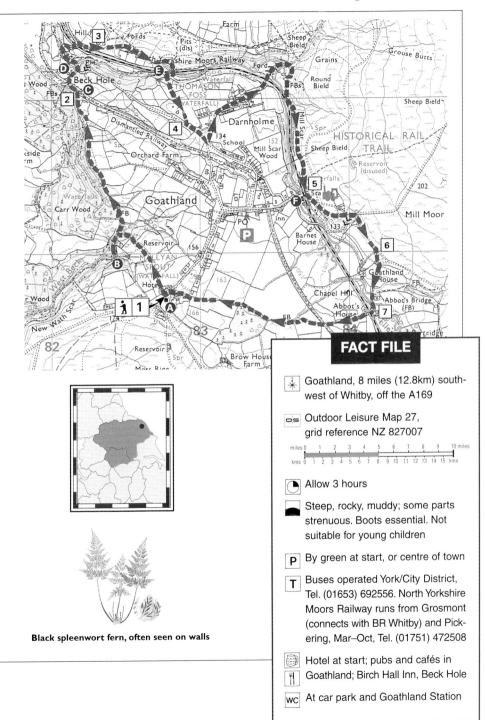

Black spleenwort fern, often seen on walls

FACT FILE

✱ Goathland, 8 miles (12.8km) south-west of Whitby, off the A169

▱ Outdoor Leisure Map 27, grid reference NZ 827007

miles 0 1 2 3 4 5 6 7 8 9 10 miles
kms 0 1 2 3 4 5 6 7 8 9 10 11 12 13 14 15 kms

◑ Allow 3 hours

▬ Steep, rocky, muddy; some parts strenuous. Boots essential. Not suitable for young children

P By green at start, or centre of town

T Buses operated York/City District, Tel. (01653) 692556. North Yorkshire Moors Railway runs from Grosmont (connects with BR Whitby) and Pickering, Mar–Oct, Tel. (01751) 472508

▥ Hotel at start; pubs and cafés in Goathland; Birch Hall Inn, Beck Hole

WC At car park and Goathland Station

The Grosmont–Pickering Steam Railway

One of the railway's fiery leviathans pulls into Goathland Station, evoking memories of the golden days of steam.

There are few more pleasant ways of viewing this delightful part of the North York Moors than from a train steaming along the line between Grosmont and Pickering, which winds through wooded valleys and across open moorland. There is a steam-hauled service from spring through to the autumn, with special excursions through the year.

The history of the railway started in 1831, when George Stephenson was asked to build a horse tramroad between Whitby and Pickering. The line was needed to transport coal, limestone and timber.

Work proceeded quickly, considering the terrain. A 120-yard (108m) tunnel had to be constructed at Grosmont. The incline between Beck Hole and Goathland was another challenge, and problems were posed by the deep Fen Bog at the top of the incline. The line was finally opened on 26 May 1836.

The costs of construction meant there were financial problems from the start. It was purchased by the York & North Midland Railway in 1844, and by 1846 there was a steam railway between Pickering and Whitby.

In the twentieth century, as private motoring increased and the Beeching Plan ravaged the railways in the 1960s, the line looked set to close. It was saved by the formation of the North York Moors Railway Preservation Society. After much hard work, the Grosmont–Pickering stretch was reopened in 1973. Since then, it has proved one of North Yorkshire's most popular attractions.

Ancient Lanes

Picture-postcard villages on the edge of the North York Moors

This view of heather-covered moors can be seen from near Spaunton.

The pretty villages of Hutton-le-Hole and Lastingham mark the southern edge of the North York Moors, the largest area of heather moorland in England. To the south of the villages lie cultivated fields.

Tamed over the centuries, this farmland contrasts sharply with the wild moors, which form a magnificent backdrop to these picturesque settlements, particularly in late summer, when vast rolling tracts of purple stretch away to the horizon.

The walk begins in Hutton-le-Hole, then follows the edge of the moorland, where upland birds including curlew, red grouse and lapwing live. Insects such as the northern eggar moth and green hairstreak butterfly can also be seen.

29

THE WALK

HUTTON-LE-HOLE–LASTINGHAM–APPLETON-LE-MOORS
The walk starts from the car park at
the north end of Hutton-le-Hole.

1 Right out of car park along lane. At a fork, right and continue a mile (1.6km). At junction, take right fork uphill, signed Appleton-le-Moors. Beyond farm on right, follow lane to left, through Spaunton **A** to a junction.

2 Turn left, downhill, to Lastingham. The church **B** and pub **C** are to left as you enter village. Continue on main street to T-junction. Right, and follow road as it bends left.

3 After last house on right, turn right over stile into field. Before end of field, over stile to right into wood. Cross bridge. At end of wood, cross stile into long, narrow field. At far end, go through gate, along edge of two fields, woodland to right, to lane.

4 Right; follow lane as it twice bends right. At T-junction, left to Appleton-le-Moors **D**.

Opposite church, go down track at side of hotel.

5 When track bends left round garden wall, go straight on to crossing of tracks. Right through gate along track through long field. At end, left along bridleway. Through gate, follow path beside trees to end of field.

6 Through marked gate to wood; follow path along edge. Path becomes a track. Where farm track joins on left, bear right, then straight. At end of field on left, follow track left. Continue as track goes right, to wood. After gate, track swings left. At bottom of hill, bear right to road.

7 Right; through village, with museum **E** to right. Right, opposite gift shop, to car park.

FACT FILE

⚹ Hutton-le-Hole, 7 miles (11.2km) north-west of Pickering, off A170

▭ Outdoor Leisure Map 26, grid reference SE 704901

miles 0	1	2	3	4	5	6	7	8	9	10 miles
kms 0	1 2 3 4 5 6 7 8 9 10 11 12 13 14 15 kms									

◐ Allow 4 hours

▬ Mostly level lanes and good tracks

P Large car park at the start

🏠 H. -le-Hole, Lastingham, A. -le-Moors

🍴 Hutton-le-Hole, Lastingham

WC At start and Ryedale Folk Museum

I Tourist Inf., Tel. (01751) 417367

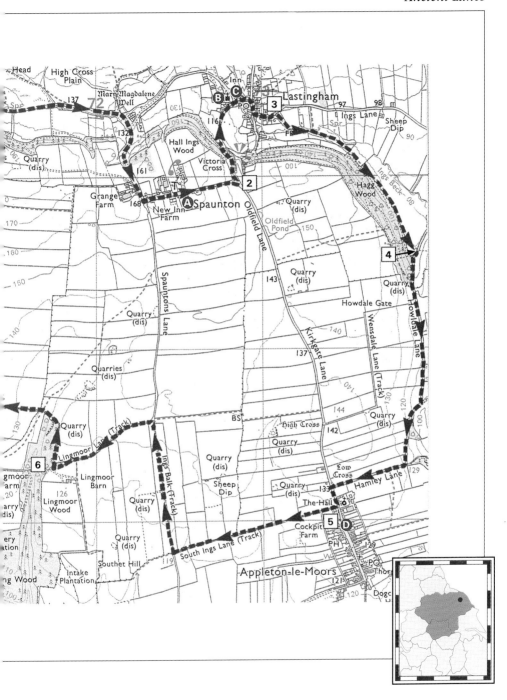

The Ryedale Folk Museum

The blacksmith's shop at the museum has been reconstructed to look much as it would have done in the 19th century.

This fascinating museum opened in 1964 and occupies a 2½-acre (1-ha) site in Hutton-le-Hole.

The entrance building was originally an 18th-century stables and a barn. It houses an exhibition of old domestic and farming implements. More farming machinery, including a steam-driven threshing machine and a horse-wheel, are to be found in other parts of the museum.

Behind the entrance building is a row of shops and workshops, and a smithy. Here, it is possible to step back in time and enter the premises of a chemist, cooper, tinsmith, shoe-maker, cabinet maker, saddler or wheelwright, or inspect the iron-making equipment of a small foundry.

Scattered round the site are several houses. These include a 500-year-old cruck house from Stangend, Danby, a thatched cottage with its interior in the style of an old farm cottage, and a 16th-century manor house. In this, every September, the World Merrills Championship is staged. This ancient board game, also known as Nine Men's Morris, has long been popular in the region.

Children are always drawn to the witch's den (complete with witch and black cat), the bow-top gypsy caravan, and the village stocks. Other exhibits include an Elizabethan glass furnace, an Edwardian photographer's studio and a collection of objects found at local archaeological digs.

Demonstrations of country crafts are often staged, and you may be lucky enough to see a display of maypole dancing by local children.

Yorkshire's Famous Moor

A walk across open moorland
on the edge of Ilkley town

Ilkley Moor is an expanse of heather, bilberry, bracken, crag and open heath.

Ilkley Moor is a nationally famous area of open moorland. Its fame is in part due to the Victorian popular song 'On Ilkla' Moor Baht 'At' — often considered Yorkshire's national anthem.

The history of the town of Ilkley **Ⓐ** goes back to Iron Age times. Then it was a riverside settlement by a ford (Llecan), where the Romans built a camp (Olicana)

to guard their road crossing of the Wharfe, downstream from the present 17th-century packhorse bridge. Remains of the camp can be seen behind Ilkley's medieval church, which has three magnificent carved Anglo-Viking gravestone crosses inside the tower.

The Tudor Manor house nearby contains many Roman archaeological finds, and

Continued on p. 36➡

THE WALK

ILKLEY–ILKLEY MOOR
The walk begins in Ilkley.

1 From the central car park or railway station cross to Brook Street (main shopping street). At the top of the road there is a T-junction with The Grove. Look for phone boxes on Wells Promenade (which leads off the junction). Opposite are central gardens. Follow path to left of stream through gardens.

2 Cross to right-hand side of stream over bridge and exit from park at gate in top right-hand corner. Cross road and keep in same direction along Linnburn Mews, an unsurfaced road.

3 Go through gate at road end, go ahead past rear entrance to the college, through pedestrian gate right to path along right bank of the stream along a shallow ravine.

4 Turn left away from the cattle grid and immediately right into road at front of Ilkley College **B**. Keep ahead.

5 Turn left at the No Through Road sign and keep ahead up road towards moor.

6 Just by the sheep warning sign, take a grassy path right over bridge; leads to track at moor edge above houses and reservoir.

7 Where path crosses bridge and dips to pedestrian gate on right, enter the wood called Heber's Ghyll **C**. Follow path along top of wood past stone shelter to gate back onto moor.

8 Face right (ignore gap stile) and take path forking left of stile, through heather, which dips over shallow stream and bears right. The path then joins the main path. Head for boulder (the Swastika Stone **D**) on the moor edge, enclosed behind tall metal fence.

9 Follow higher level path, through the bracken and heather, crossing two wooden footbridges. Keep ahead until the path joins a metalled road. Turn left downhill for about 220 yards (200m).

10 Look for narrow path on the right which starts by a large rowan tree. This follows shallow hollow, parallel to road, then swings right to meet track to White Wells **E**.

11 From White Wells, take path on right below pools, descending the moor to pass edge of The Tarn **F**. Turn left along metalled track past paddling pool to Wells Promenade, down to centre of Ilkley and start of walk.

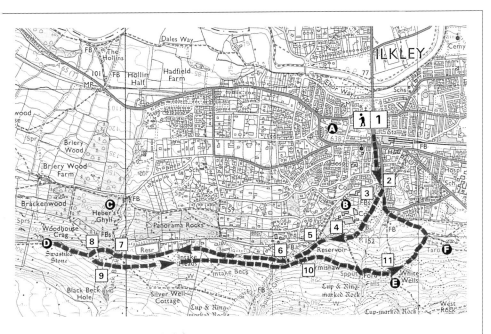

Blackbird's nest with speckled eggs

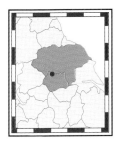

FACT FILE

☀ Ilkley, 10 miles (16km) north of Bradford

▱ Pathfinder 671 (SE 04/14), grid reference SE 116476

miles	0	1	2	3	4	5	6	7	8	9	10 miles
kms	0	1 2 3 4 5	6 7 8 9 10 11 12 13 14 15 kms

◑ 2½ hours

▬ Can be very muddy in places with fairly steep climbs

P Large central car park behind Brook Street, Ilkley

T Frequent train services to Ilkley from Leeds or Bradford (Forster Square). Bus services from Leeds, Bradford, Skipton and Keighley

🏠 Ilkley has a wide choice of pubs
🍴 and cafés

from the late 18th century onwards, Ilkley has enjoyed fame as a spa town.

Ilkley College **B** was originally built in 1865, as White Wells Hydropathic Hotel. This architecturally outstanding building now houses the Ilkley Campus of Bradford and the Community College.

The Swastika Stone

Further on the path comes to a narrow, wooded valley, Heber's Ghyll **C**, with its pretty ornamental paths and bridges, landscaped in typical late Victorian style. It takes its name from an old Ilkley family, the Hebers, of nearby Hollin Hall. The ghyll is noted for its ferns, oak and birch woods, and for its picturesque series of waterfalls.

On the moor itself, you can walk up to look at the mysterious Swastika Stone

The tarns on Ilkley Moor were originally natural pools.

D. The carving on this moorland boulder is in fact a 'folyfoot', which is an ancient Indo-European symbol of eternal life, and it probably dates from some 2,500–3,000 years ago. The inscription on the Stone states that there is a similar carving at Tossene, Sweden, and another at Mycene, Greece. There is a modern replica you can view alongside it.

Archaeological Riches

Ilkley Moor is particularly rich in archaeological remains, including literally scores of mysterious cup-and-ring-marked stones. It is a splendid viewpoint across Wharfedale and the Yorkshire Dales National Park.

Further east is White Wells **E**, which was built as a small bath-house in the 1760s by Squire Middleton of Ilkley. Situated over Ilkley Moor's most famous spring, it only took a few years before wealthy, gouty invalids were arriving from all over England to be taken by donkey from their Ilkley lodgings to be plunged in the spring's clear, icy waters.

White Wells has been beautifully restored, and it is open at weekends and holiday times as a small museum and tea rooms.

Below the Wells is a series of pools, including The Tarn **F**, which were landscaped in Victorian times from natural moorland pools. Much of the native moorland heather and bilberry, richly purple in late summer, has been lost through overgrazing and trampling. Over time the heather has been replaced by bracken and rough grass.

Pennine Ways

Along old trade routes and through a wooded valley

There are fine views from Heptonstall Crags down to Calderside.

Heptonstall ❶ is a historic village with a steep, winding cobbled main street. The earliest cottages date back to the 16th century.

In the 17th and 18th centuries, when Heptonstall was at its peak as a textile community, some cottages were the homes of handloom weavers. These are distinguishable by their rows of upstairs windows, which allowed the weavers plenty of light by which to work.

As you leave the village, you pass the parish church, with a grave in the churchyard belonging to David Hartley, hanged in York in 1770 for counterfeiting gold coins. Just beyond it stand the ruins of a 15th-century chapel, near the village's Old Grammar School, founded in 1642.

Continued on p. 40➤

37

THE WALK

HEPTONSTALL–HEBDEN DALE
The walk starts in the free car park just off
the main street in Heptonstall.

1 From the car park exit, go diagonally right at the crossroads, along a lane signposted to the Museum. Go up the signposted steps to your right. Pass through a gate at the top, to find the church and the ruins of an earlier church. The Old Grammar School is on your right. Follow the path around to the left of the church. Leave the churchyard by a short path on your left, just beyond a tall brown obelisk. Turn right along the track. After 50 yards (45m), fork left. Fork right after another 50 yards (45m), signposted to the 'Calderdale Way', along the walled Eaves Lane **B**.

2 At the end of the lane, turn right, and make your way with care along the unfenced path at the top of Heptonstall Crags **C** to a lane. Turn left, downhill, for about 100 yards (90m), then bear right along the way-marked Calderdale Way. The path soon joins a grassy, walled path (Murking Lane **D**) and continues along the side of the hill.

3 At the end of the track, turn sharp right on a field-edge path. Go through two small gates and a farmyard, and turn left along a track to the village of Slack.

4 Turn left down the road through the village. Before the road junction (the site of an old finger-post **E**), take a signposted path to your right, between houses, which opens into a walled lane. At the end of the lane, bear left and zigzag downhill through woods to Hebden Water.

5 Cross the stepping stones, and go left along the riverside path to Gibson Mill **F**. Return by the same path, then continue up the hill, and bear right to follow the river. After about 1/2 mile (800m), climb up some steps. Continue along the path, which stays close to the river, until you arrive at a bridge.

6 Turn right across this bridge, then bear left past the café at Midgehole. At a fork, bear right, walk up the hill along a paved track. At a crossroads of tracks, turn left. Continue ahead, walking through the wooded hillside, until you come to a road.

7 Bear left and continue for about 50 yards (45m). Turn right up the steps signposted to Heptonstall. At a road turn right; walk on up the hill to reach Heptonstall and the car park where the walk started.

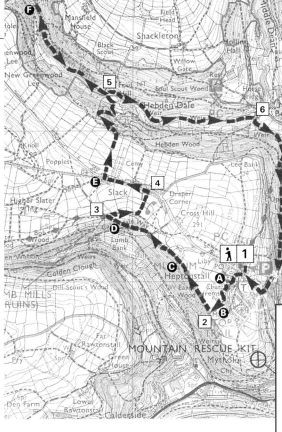

Millstones hewn from millstone grit

FACT FILE

☀ Heptonstall, 6½ miles (10.4km) west of Halifax, off the A646

▭ Pathfinder 690 (SD 82/92) or Outdoor Leisure Map 21, grid reference SD 987281

miles 0 1 2 3 4 5 6 7 8 9 10 miles
kms 0 1 2 3 4 5 6 7 8 9 10 11 12 13 14 15 kms

◔ Allow 2 hours

▬ Some steep ascents / descents. Paths good but can be slippery. One river crossing on step stones. Care needed with children, top of Heptonstall Crags. Boots essential

P Free car park at the start

T BR trains toHebden Bridge on Manchester to Leeds line; bus from station to Heptonstall

▦ The Cross Inn and the White Lion pub in Heptonstall

¶ Café at Midgehole. The farm shop at Slack sells ice cream

WC Heptonstall and Midgehole

Heptonstall lies on an old route between Halifax and Burnley. The walled lane that leads out to Heptonstall Crags, Eaves Lane ❸, was once a route for packhorses and pedestrians.

Heptonstall Crags ❸ are an outcrop of gritstone. From this vantage point, there are excellent views down the Calder Valley. The stone tower visible from many locations is Stoodley Pike, erected to commemorate the Battle of Waterloo.

Down below is Colden Water. The area around here used to be owned by the monks of Fountains Abbey, and they built a number of small water-mills in the valley. The mills were later converted to steam power, but much of the early water engineering remains, now hidden in dense woods.

Murking Lane ❸, another walled and partly paved lane, is followed for a time from Heptonstall Crags. It now forms part of a long-distance footpath, the Calderdale Way. There were many such routes between mills and villages, and, at the top of this lane, there is an intersection of five of these Pennine tracks.

The route goes through Slack, where a 17th-century finger-post ❸ indicates

You can cross Hebden Water by stepping stones to walk to Gibson Mill.

'Burnly', an archaic spelling of Burnley. A lane lined with bilberry bushes leads you to a wooded ravine, and you descend to Hebden Water. The woods are a paradise, with the flora including enchanter's nightshade, wood anemones and pink campion. The treecreeper, a small, brown bird with a curved beak, probes the bark of trees here for insects.

You cross Hebden Water by stepping stones, known in these parts as 'hipping stones', and head upstream through pine woods to Gibson Mill ❸. The deserted mill is named after a cotton spinner, by the name of Abraham Gibson. The bridge here was once a tollbridge.

The route now heads back downstream. The woods are home to large wood ants, which make their nests out of the pine needles. As well as Scots pine, there are attractive mature trees including beech, birch and holly. In spring, the slopes are covered in bluebells, and you may also find wild hyacinth. At Midgehole, you cross the river by another old tollbridge, and head uphill. At the top there are fine views over Hebden Bridge. A further steep climb returns you to the start of the walk.

Summer Wine Country

A scenic walk through a deep Pennine valley

Holmfirth can be seen to great advantage from the surrounding hills.

The pennine town of Holmfirth is typical of the West Yorkshire scene, with its stone walls, steep streets and moorland setting.

Its distinctive character made it an ideal choice as a location in the popular television series 'Last of the Summer Wine', first shown in 1972. The walk includes visits to many places seen in the programme.

The town's buildings are made with local stone, and some retain weavers' windows on the upper storey; these allowed plenty of light to reach the looms.

There are several split-level houses on the hills, with the top storeys reached from an upper level. In the valleys around the town you can still see mills that were once powered by water from local streams.

41

THE WALK

HOLMFIRTH

The walk begins at the car park in Holmfirth.

1 From car park, to Huddersfield Rd; left. Along road to end of Cooper Lane **Ⓐ**, on right. Past lights to museum **Ⓑ**. On to shop **Ⓒ**, on left.

2 Left to Upper Bridge in Hollowgate **Ⓓ**. Follow to left into Victoria Sq. and church in Towngate. Right just before church to courtyard. Café **Ⓔ** on right. Up steps by church on left; left, then right to steps to Bunkers Hill. At junction, back right to next junction.

3 Left and up road; take first road, hard back left, before Rose Cott. Pass below Moor View Cott.; up twisty road to junction at top of New Laithe Lane. Left, then right on grassy track.

4 Route turns right through gateway; follow lane a little to see view. Return to gate. With wall right, turn right then left to lane. Past farm, fork right to lane. Left to road.

5 Right, then first left down lane. Almost immediate left turn past gate, to follow footpath. 10 yards (9m) on, left down path to track. Left down track to estate; Right through estate.

6 Choose to stay on pavement to junction and right turn to Green Hill Bank Rd; or turn right to play field, left behind houses. At end of field, path by fence to steps to Green Hill Bank Rd; right.

7 Up road. At top of hill, opp. No. 47, left fork down lane. At bend, ahead through stile by gate, follow path. Pass into wood, path to mill. Left; right past buildings.

8 Cross stream at mill entrance; right in front of houses, by stream. Track forks left past ruin;

on, above stream, to mill. Steps **Ⓕ** to left, to road.

9 Right; soon fork right to Jackson Bridge.

10 Right to Inn **Ⓖ**. Take Scholes Rd, valley to right. After ½ mile (800m), left, Paris Rd.

11 Right up Cherry Tree Wk. Second turn left to cul-de-sac; right on signed path. Through stile, then another in field corner. Keep wall left, past hamlet. Cross two stiles; another between gates. Three more, to lane. Left to road.

12 Right on path by road. At fork, left; down road back to town.

13 Before big road, right; steps to square. Left; right to Towngate; on to pillar **Ⓗ**. Pass toilets, left past P.O. At end of street, right on path. Second bridge to car park.

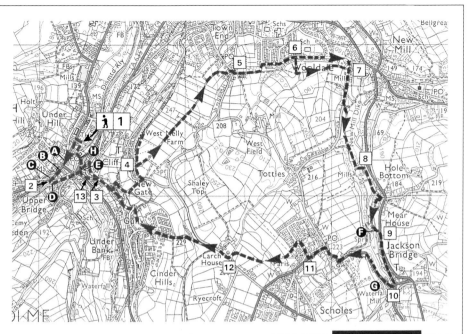

Curlew, with long, curved bill

FACT FILE

☀ Holmfirth, 6½ miles (10km) south of Huddersfield on A6024 and A635

▱ Pathfinder 714 (SE 00/10), grid reference SE 143083

◑ Allow 4 hours

◣ Walking boots recommended

P Car park behind the Postcard Inn, Huddersfield Road, Holmfirth

T Bus to and from Huddersfield, Leeds and Marsden

🍴 Inns and cafés in Holmfirth

WC Holmfirth, near post office

⊓ Holmfirth Postcard Museum open Mon–Sat, 10.00 am–5.00 pm, Sun 1.00–5.00 pm

Comic Cards

COUPLE HERE READY FOR BEDDING OUT BERT !

Holmfirth is home to J Bamforth & Company, the creators of the classic saucy postcard. The humour is based on the traditional 'double entendre'.

Many of the postcards that are so much a feature of every seaside town are printed in Holmfirth by J Bamforth & Company. The company was founded in 1870 by James Bamforth, an artist, who produced the backdrops for many of the cards and also for lantern slides.

Shortly after the turn of the century, the company began making comedy films. They were filmed around Holmfirth, and local people were used as actors.

The company also began producing cards, often in sets of three, showing sentimental scenes and including the words of popular songs. During World War I, cards featuring popular songs such as 'My Hero' and 'Goodbye Dolly Gray' sold well to people wanting to express their feelings to volunteers fighting on the Western Front.

As the postcards with songs declined in popularity, the company switched to comic postcards, many of which have become classics of their kind. In 1975, Kirklees Metropolitan Council was given a collection of cards that had been amassed by Major Robert W Scherer, of Florida. He had at first been interested in those depicting hymns and songs, but then expanded his collection to include all Bamforth's postcards.

Today the company still produces their comic cards, as well as greetings cards and calendars.

Index